Torque brims with excitement perfect for thrill-seekers of all kinds. Discover daring survival skills, explore uncharted worlds, and marvel at mighty engines and extreme sports. In *Torque* books, anything can happen. Are you ready?

This edition first published in 2025 by Bellwether Media, Inc.

No part of this publication may be reproduced in whole or in part without written permission of the publisher. For information regarding permission, write to Bellwether Media, Inc., Attention: Permissions Department, 6012 Blue Circle Drive, Minnetonka, MN 55343.

Library of Congress Cataloging-in-Publication Data

Names: Golkar, Golriz, author.
Title: Katie Ledecky / by Golriz Golkar.
Description: Minneapolis, MN : Bellwether Media, 2025. | Series: Torque. Sports superstars | Includes bibliographical references and index. | Audience: Ages 7-12 | Audience: Grades 4-6 | Summary: "Engaging images accompany information about Katie Ledecky. The combination of high-interest subject matter and light text is intended for students in grades 3 through 7"– Provided by publisher.
Identifiers: LCCN 2024009927 (print) | LCCN 2024009928 (ebook) | ISBN 9798893040357 (library binding) | ISBN 9781644879733 (ebook)
Subjects: LCSH: Ledecky, Katie, 1997–Juvenile literature. | Women swimmers–United States–Biography–Juvenile literature. | Swimmers–United States–Biography–Juvenile literature. | Women Olympic athletes–United States–Biography–Juvenile literature. | Olympic athletes–United States–Biography–Juvenile literature.
Classification: LCC GV838.L43 G65 2025 (print) | LCC GV838.L43 (ebook)
LC record available at https://lccn.loc.gov/2024009927
LC ebook record available at https://lccn.loc.gov/2024009928

Text copyright © 2025 by Bellwether Media, Inc. TORQUE and associated logos are trademarks and/or registered trademarks of Bellwether Media, Inc. Bellwether Media is a division of Chrysalis Education Group.

Editor: Kieran Downs   Designer: Gabriel Hilger

Printed in the United States of America, North Mankato, MN.

TABLE OF CONTENTS

SPLASH!!!	4
WHO IS KATIE LEDECKY?	6
A RISING SWIM STAR	8
SWIMMING CHAMPION	12
LEDECKY'S FUTURE	20
GLOSSARY	22
TO LEARN MORE	23
INDEX	24

SPLASH!!!

It is the 2012 London **Olympic Games**. The 800-meter **freestyle** event is about to start. The whistle blows. The eight swimmers dive into the water. Katie Ledecky races ahead of the others.

She reaches the wall and flips. Ledecky is in the lead! Ledecky finishes the race in just over eight minutes. She wins the gold medal!

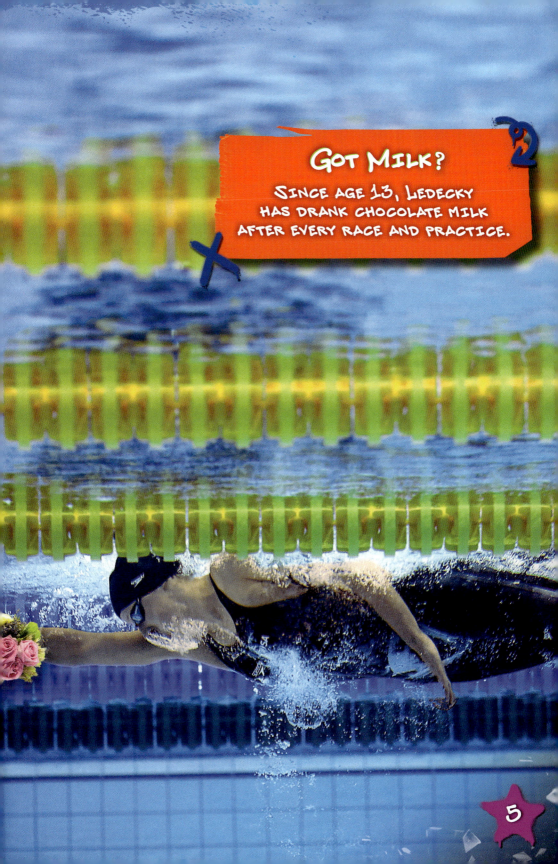

GOT MILK?

Since age 13, Ledecky has drank chocolate milk after every race and practice.

WHO IS KATIE LEDECKY?

Katie Ledecky is a swimmer. She has set many freestyle swimming records. She has also won many Olympic medals. Ledecky has won more medals than any other female swimmer in the world.

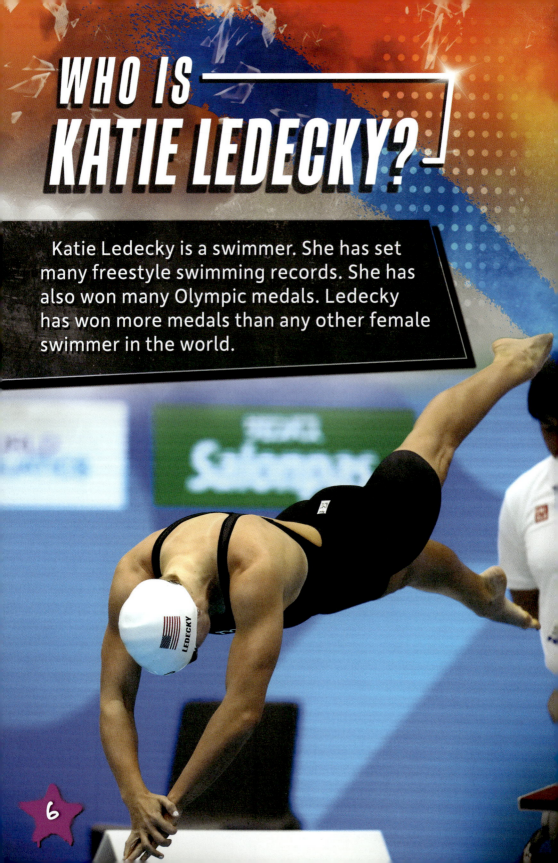

KATIE LEDECKY

BIRTHDAY March 17, 1997

HOMETOWN Bethesda, Maryland

STROKE freestyle

HEIGHT 6 feet

JOINED Team USA in 2012

Ledecky works with companies that make sports products. She also supports **charities** that help people in need.

A RISING SWIM STAR

Ledecky started swimming at age 6. She joined a summer swim **league** with her older brother. Ledecky started training with Nation's Capital Swim Club in 2009. Her new coach taught her how to improve her stroke.

LEDECKY AND HER BROTHER

U.S. JUNIOR CHAMPIONSHIPS

Ledecky became a strong swimmer. At age 14, Ledecky won three freestyle events at the U.S. Junior **Championships**.

Ledecky swam in the 2012 U.S. **Olympic Trials**. She was only 15 years old. She won the 800-meter freestyle. This won her a spot on Team USA. She became their youngest member.

Ledecky swam well at the 2012 London Olympic Games. She won the gold medal in the 800-meter freestyle!

2012 LONDON OLYMPIC GAMES

FAVORITES

FOOD	INSTRUMENT	TV SHOW	SPORTS TEAM
 Reese's Peanut Butter Cups	piano	 Blue Bloods	New York Islanders

Training Time

Ledecky trains in the pool for about 20 hours per week. She also spends 5 hours per week at the gym.

SWIMMING CHAMPION

Ledecky won four gold medals at the 2013 World Championships. She also set two world records. In 2014, Ledecky won five gold medals at the Pan Pacific Championships.

2014 PAN PACIFIC CHAMPIONSHIPS

2015 WORLD CHAMPIONSHIPS

In 2015, she returned to the World Championships. She became the first female swimmer to win four individual freestyle events at the World Championships.

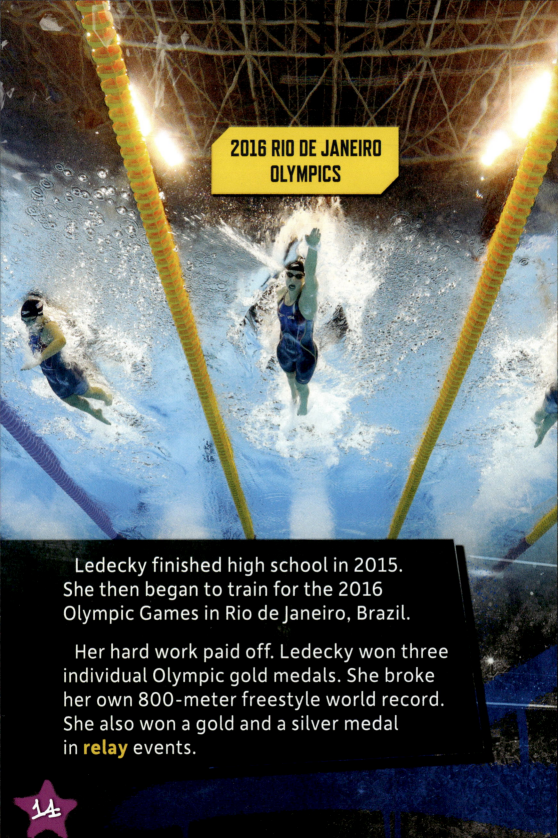

2016 RIO DE JANEIRO OLYMPICS

Ledecky finished high school in 2015. She then began to train for the 2016 Olympic Games in Rio de Janeiro, Brazil.

Her hard work paid off. Ledecky won three individual Olympic gold medals. She broke her own 800-meter freestyle world record. She also won a gold and a silver medal in **relay** events.

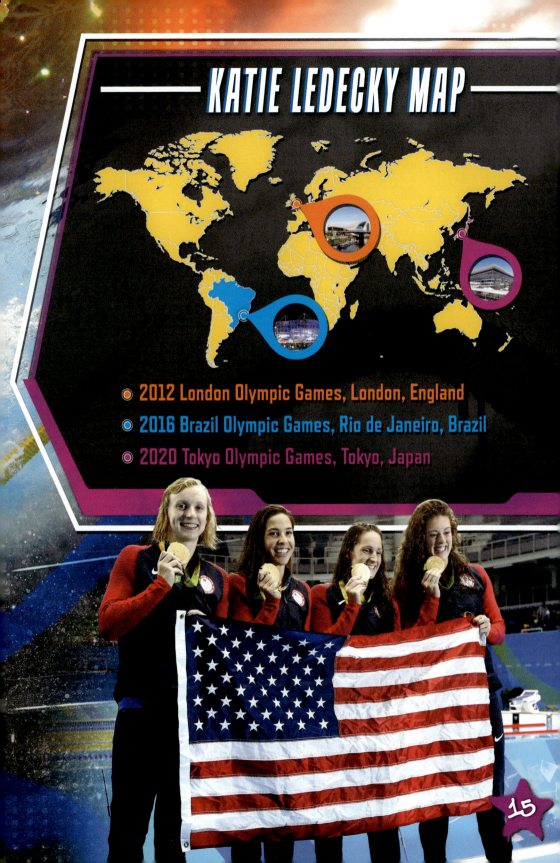

Ledecky began studying at Stanford University in 2016. She swam on the Stanford swim team for two seasons. She helped her team win **National Collegiate Athletic Association** (NCAA) and **conference** championships. She won eight individual NCAA medals. She was also named an NCAA **All-American**.

Ledecky won five gold medals at the 2017 World Championships. In 2018, she won five Pan Pacific Championship medals.

2017 NCAA CHAMPIONSHIPS

2018 PAN PACIFIC CHAMPIONSHIPS

TROPHY SHELF

Olympic gold medals

Olympic silver medals

World Championship gold medals

NCAA Championships

NCAA All-Americans

17

Ledecky won three medals at the 2019 World Championships. She also swam in the 2020 Tokyo Olympic Games. Ledecky became the first woman to win the new 1500-meter freestyle event. She won four medals at the games, including two golds.

In 2021, Ledecky graduated from Stanford as a top student and athlete.

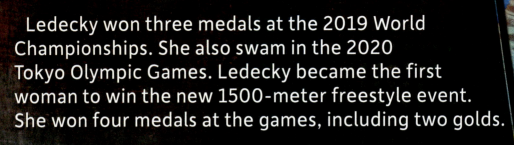

2019 WORLD CHAMPIONSHIPS

TIMELINE

— 2012 —
Ledecky wins her first Olympic gold medal

— 2013 —
Ledecky wins four gold medals at the 2013 World Championships

— 2014 —
Ledecky wins five gold medals at the Pan Pacific Championships

18

2020 TOKYO OLYMPIC GAMES

Olympic Champion

At the 2020 Tokyo Olympic Games, Ledecky became the first female swimmer to win seven Olympic gold medals!*

— 2016 —
Ledecky wins five medals at the Rio de Janeiro Olympic Games

— 2021 —
Ledecky wins four medals at the Tokyo Olympic Games

— 2023 —
Ledecky sets a new world record for the most World Championship wins

LEDECKY'S FUTURE

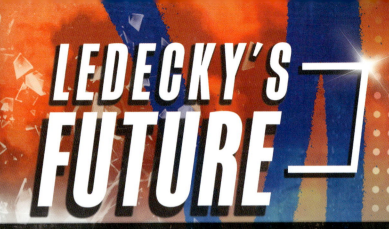

Ledecky won four gold medals at the 2022 World Championships. She won two more in 2023. This makes her the swimmer with the most individual World Championship gold medals in history!

GIVING BIKES

Ledecky works with groups that give bicycles to people in need!

2023 WORLD CHAMPIONSHIPS

Ledecky gives back to the community. She works to help children get **STEM** education. She plans to swim at the 2024 Paris Olympic Games. She hopes to win more medals!

GLOSSARY

All-American—a title given to outstanding young athletes in different sports

championships—contests to decide the best team or person

charities—organizations that help others in need

conference—related to a grouping of teams that often compete against each other

freestyle—a style of swimming in which swimmers can choose the stroke they use

league—a group of teams or individuals that regularly compete against one another

National Collegiate Athletic Association—a group in charge of student athletes at colleges in the United States; the National Collegiate Athletic Association is often called the NCAA.

Olympic Games—worldwide summer or winter sports contests held in a different country every four years

Olympic Trials—contests held in certain sports to decide who will be on the Olympic team

relay—related to a race between teams in which each team member completes one part of the race course

STEM—a group of school subjects; STEM stands for science, technology, engineering, and mathematics.

TO LEARN MORE

AT THE LIBRARY

Corey, Shana. *Katie Ledecky: A Little Golden Book Biography*. New York, N.Y.: Golden Books, 2024.

Fishman, Jon M. *Katie Ledecky*. Minneapolis, Minn.: Lerner Publications, 2021.

Golkar, Golriz. *Sunisa Lee*. Minneapolis, Minn.: Bellwether Media, 2025.

ON THE WEB

FACTSURFER

Factsurfer.com gives you a safe, fun way to find more information.

1. Go to www.factsurfer.com

2. Enter "Katie Ledecky" into the search box and click.

3. Select your book cover to see a list of related content.

INDEX

All-American, 16
charities, 7, 21
childhood, 5, 8, 9, 10, 14
family, 8
favorites, 11
freestyle, 4, 6, 9, 10, 13, 14, 18
future, 21
map, 15
medals, 4, 6, 10, 12, 14, 16, 18, 19, 20, 21
NCAA Championships, 16
Olympic Games, 4, 6, 10, 14, 18, 19, 21
Pan Pacific Championships, 12, 16, 17

profile, 7
records, 6, 12, 13, 14, 18, 19, 20
Stanford University, 16, 18
STEM, 21
Team USA, 10
timeline, 18–19
training, 8, 11, 14
trophy shelf, 17
U.S. Junior Championships, 9
U.S. Olympic Trials, 10
World Championships, 12, 13, 16, 18, 20, 21

The images in this book are reproduced through the courtesy of: KYDPL KYODO/ AP Images, front cover; Insidefoto di andrea staccioli/ Alamy, p. 3; UPI/ Alamy Stock Photo, p. 4; Robert Beck/ Contributor/ Getty, pp. 4-5; Lee Jin-man/ AP Images, p. 6; sharpener, p. 7 (American flag); Eugene Hoshiko/ AP Images, p. 7 (Katie Ledecky); Variety/ Contributor/ Getty, p. 8; Mo Khursheed/ AP Images, p. 9; Zuma Press, Inc./ Alamy, p. 10; Jennifer Wallace, p. 11 (Reese's Peanut Butter Cups); Venus Angel, p. 11 (piano); Cinematic/ Alamy, p. 11 (*Blue Bloods*); New York Islanders/ Wikipedia, p. 11 (New York Islanders); Tony Marshall/ AP Images, p. 11 (Katie Ledecky); Rick Rycroft/ AP Images, p. 12; Aflo Co. Ltd./ Alamy, pp. 12-13; David J. Phillip/ AP Images, pp. 14, 21; AC Manley, p. 15 (London Olympic Games); Shahjehan, p. 15 (Rio Olympic Games); Ryosei Watanabe, p. 15 (Tokyo Olympic Games); Daniel A. Anderson/ AP Images, p. 15 (Katie Ledecky at the Rio Olympic Games); Jeffrey Brown/ AP Images, p. 16; Koji Sasahara/ AP Images, p. 17; Mark Schiefelbein/ AP Images, p. 18 (2019 World Championships); Tony Baggett, p. 18 (2012); Daniel Ochoa de Olza/ AP Images, p. 18 (2013); Jeff Roberson/ AP Images, pp. 18-19; Michael Sohn/ AP Images, p. 19 (2016); fifg, p. 19 (2021); Miho Ikeya/ AP Images, p. 20; Michael Conroy/ AP Images, p. 23.